UNIVERSAL SYNCHRONISM

In the Digital Age

Katia Doria Fonseca Vasconcelos

Dedication

With immense gratitude, I present this new chapter of the literary journey, "Universal Synchronism," and share it with all of you, dear readers.

May this book, "Universal Synchronism," be a source of inspiration and reflection, leading you on a journey filled with discoveries and learning. May each page of this work awaken curiosity, empathy, and the desire to explore the universe of the human heart and the complexities of existence.

With dedication and passion for writing about balance, technology, and personal development, I hope this book can touch your hearts and inspire a pursuit of continuous improvement and an understanding of the importance of respecting differences while nurturing love and kindness in our lives.

Thank you for accompanying me on this literary journey, and together, may we continue to explore new horizons of wisdom and self-awareness.

With affection,

Katia Doria Fonseca Vasconcelos

Introduction

In the digital age we live in, we are witnesses to an unprecedented technological revolution. The current society is increasingly interconnected, with people around the world communicating instantaneously and sharing information on a global scale. Advanced technology permeates every aspect of our lives, from work to entertainment, and has deeply impacted the way we perceive the world.

In this book, "Universal Synchronism: In the Digital Age," we will explore the fascinating intersection between technological evolution and the quantum principles of physics, which have the potential to open new horizons for understanding ourselves and the universe we inhabit. This work aims to be not only a scientific account but also a philosophical journey in search of a more comprehensive vision of our existence.

The Digital Age and Interconnection

The digital age has brought about a growing interconnection between humans and technology. The internet and social media have become the pillars of modern communication, allowing information to flow freely and instantly between people from different cultures and contexts. Digital communication transcends geographical and cultural barriers, creating a global network of interaction and knowledge-sharing.

Scientific research has shown the impact of this interconnection on how we perceive the world and on our cognition. Studies on the influence of social media on interpersonal relationships indicate that virtual communication can affect our emotions and the construction of our digital identities. Additionally, the advent of virtual reality has deepened our ability to immerse ourselves in digital experiences, expanding our perception of reality.

The Importance of Philosophical and Scientific Approaches

When addressing the topic of Universal Synchronism, it is essential to recognize the relevance of both philosophy and science. Throughout history, philosophy has been a powerful tool for exploring fundamental questions about human existence, the universe, and our relationship with it. It invites us to question and reflect on the nature of reality, our perceptions, and the structures that shape our beliefs.

Science, on the other hand, offers an objective and methodological approach to investigate the phenomena of the natural world and the cosmos. Based on empirical evidence and rigorous experiments, science allows us to understand the mechanisms and underlying patterns that govern the functioning of the universe. Quantum physics, in particular, has stood out as a field that challenges our conventional understanding of reality.

By combining these two perspectives, philosophy and science, we seek a holistic approach to explore the concept of Universal Synchronism. It is not about blindly accepting esoteric theories or unfounded conjectures but rather applying a critical and informed view to understand the possible interconnections between technological advancements, quantum physics, and our own existence.

Therefore, we invite the reader to embark on this journey towards Universal Synchronism, exploring the frontiers of knowledge and opening the mind to new possibilities. The next chapter will take us on a deeper exploration of the fundamentals of quantum physics and how it challenges our traditional conceptions of the universe.

SUMÁRIO

THE QUANTUM REVOLUTION AND ITS INFLUENCE ON OUR PERCEPTION OF REALITY

The Quantum Revolution: Quantum physics is undoubtedly one of the most extraordinary achievements of human thought, challenging our conventional understanding of the universe. In this chapter, we will delve into the fundamentals of quantum physics and explore how it has profoundly revolutionized our view of the world and ourselves.

What Is Quantum Physics?

Quantum physics is the fundamental theory that describes the behavior of subatomic particles, such as electrons and photons, as well as the fundamental forces of nature, including gravity and electromagnetism. Its development in the early 20th century was a response to the challenges presented by phenomena that classical physics could not fully explain.

Unlike classical physics, which describes the macroscopic world with deterministic laws, quantum physics is inherently probabilistic. It introduces revolutionary concepts, such as superposition, where a particle can exist in multiple states simultaneously, and entanglement, where two particles can remain interconnected in an inseparable way, even when separated by large distances.

The Observer and Particle Behavior

One of the most intriguing aspects of quantum physics is the role of the observer in the process. According to the theory, the mere observation of a particle can directly influence its behavior. The iconic double-slit experiment, for example, reveals that a particle, such as an electron or a photon, can behave both as a wave and a particle, depending on whether it is being observed or not.

This wave-particle duality challenges our intuition about how the world should function. The act of observation appears to have the power to influence the reality of the particle, shedding light on profound philosophical questions about the nature of existence and the intricate relationship between the observer and the observed.

Decoherence and the Metric of Reality:

Decoherence is a central concept in quantum physics that explains how particles lose their quantum characteristics when interacting with the environment, becoming part of classical reality. This transition is essential to our understanding of objective reality in the macroscopic world, where objects exhibit predictable and deterministic behavior.

Decoherence plays a crucial role in the metric of our experience of the world. The interactions between quantum particles and the environment trigger an effect of indirect measurement, fundamental to the perception we have of the external reality. It is through this mechanism that quantum physics connects to the macroscopic world, providing the basis for understanding how our reality emerges from the intricate underlying quantum interactions.

Understanding decoherence allows us to explain why we do not perceive quantum superpositions or entanglements in everyday life. Through this analysis, quantum physics reveals itself as a scientific revolution that challenges our classical view of the world while opening us up to new reflections on the relationship between objective reality and our perception of it.

THE NEED FOR METRICS IN PERCEPTION OF REALITY

As human beings, we rely on metrics to comprehend and interpret the vast world around us. Our senses are limited, and to overcome this limitation, we employ tools and instruments that allow us to measure and quantify aspects of the universe that we cannot perceive directly. These metrics provide solid foundations for our understanding of objective reality, enabling us to make informed decisions in our daily lives.

The quest for precise and reliable metrics has been a constant in the history of science. Galileo Galilei, a prominent figure in scientific history, was one of the pioneers in using mathematics to describe the motion of celestial bodies, providing a quantitative framework for classical physics. This metric approach was of fundamental importance for the development of modern science.

However, quantum physics has presented significant challenges to our need for precise metrics. Quantum phenomena, such as wave-particle duality and entanglement, do not easily fit into our classical understanding of the world, where particles are described by well-defined positions and states. The probabilistic nature of quantum physics makes it difficult to predict the behavior of subatomic particles with certainty.

Nevertheless, quantum physics has also bestowed upon us a new metric approach to understanding reality. Instead of confining ourselves to classical metrics, quantum physics invites us to explore the probabilistic nature of quantum systems. Rather than determining precise positions and states for particles, we work with probability distributions that reflect our inherent uncertainty about quantum reality.

This probabilistic metric approach is particularly relevant when dealing with complex systems and quantum interactions. Through advanced techniques such as matrix quantum mechanics and second quantization, we can describe systems with multiple particles and entangled states, providing a more comprehensive and robust view of quantum reality.

Thus, this new metric approach of quantum physics challenges us to rethink our classical intuitions and invites us to explore the complex and interconnected nature of the universe. By accepting the probabilistic and indeterminate nature of quantum reality, we recognize that our perception of reality is constructed through intricate interactions between the observer and the observed.

This quantum revolution has profound implications for our understanding of time and space in the digital era. Information technology, with its processing power and connectivity, offers a new perspective for applying the probabilistic metrics of quantum physics in our daily lives.

In the digital age, the ability to collect and analyze vast amounts of data allows us to explore complex phenomena and create probabilistic models to describe interconnected systems. This enables us to advance fields such as artificial intelligence and machine learning, where the uncertainties and randomness of quantum phenomena can be used to improve algorithms and make more informed decisions.

Furthermore, the digital age allows us to share information and knowledge instantly and globally, bringing humanity closer together and creating collective awareness of the discoveries of quantum physics and its philosophical implications. Global collaboration and widespread access to information enable more brilliant minds to collaborate in unraveling the mysteries of quantum physics and its influence on our perception of reality.

As we delve deeper into this intersection between the quantum revolution and the digital era, we are led to question the limits of our understanding, both of the quantum microcosm and the digital macrocosm. New perspectives emerge, expanding our comprehension of existence, the universe, and our relationship with it.

In this context, our book "Universal Synchronism: In the Digital Era" seeks to explore these fascinating connections between the quantum revolution and digital transformation, providing a journey full of discoveries and reflections on the nature of reality, perception of the world around us, and the role of the human being as an observer and participant in this intricate cosmic fabric.

Understanding the influence of quantum physics on our perception of reality is essential for embracing the complexity of existence and embarking on a quest for deeper and more meaningful knowledge. Only by integrating these scientific advancements with ancient wisdom and collective consciousness can we glimpse a Universal Synchronism that transcends the boundaries of knowledge and leads us to new horizons of understanding and evolution.

Therefore, I invite the reader to accompany the journey that begins in this book, where we unite the quantum revolution with the digital era, exploring the frontiers of knowledge and contemplating the infinite universe of possibilities that reveal themselves before our eyes. Let us embark together on this quest for Universal Synchronism, toward a deeper and enlightened understanding of our existence in this vast cosmos.

THE PROFOUND INTERCONNECTION BETWEEN MIND AND UNIVERSE

In this chapter, we will delve into the depths of Universal Synchronism, a philosophical approach that leads us to the understanding of how everything in the universe is intricately interconnected, transcending the boundaries of time and space. Grounded in the principles of quantum physics, this concept offers a unique perspective on the nature of reality and the influence of the human mind in the manifestation of the world around us.

THE QUANTUM BASIS OF UNIVERSAL SYNCHRONISM

Quantum physics reveals to us that reality is much more fluid and mutable than we imagined. Subatomic particles, such as electrons and photons, can exist in states of superposition, assuming multiple possibilities simultaneously until observed. This probabilistic nature of reality, coupled with the phenomenon of quantum entanglement, where distant particles remain instantaneously interconnected, transcends the boundaries of conventional perception.

It is in this context that Universal Synchronism finds its foundation: the profound and inseparable interconnection of all things in the universe. The fundamental elements of the cosmos are intrinsically linked, regardless of distance and time, suggesting an invisible web that permeates all existence. Quantum physics allows us to glimpse this web, where each event is entangled with all others.

DECOHERENCE AND THE CREATION OF REALITY

Through the process of decoherence, quantum physics shows us how reality materializes through observation. When a particle is observed, it "decides" in which state to manifest, and all other possibilities vanish. This act of observation by the human mind is fundamental to the creation of our reality. The way we interpret and ascribe meaning to events around us shapes the reality we experience.

Universal Synchronism recognizes the human mind as an active element in this process. Individual perception and cognition create a unique lens through which we interpret and interact with the world. Our experiences, thoughts, and emotions influence how reality unfolds before us, causing each human being to create their own foundation of reality.

SYNCHRONICITY AND THE EXPANSION OF CONSCIOUSNESS

In this paradigm of Universal Synchronism, synchronicity takes center stage. Synchronicity is the occurrence of seemingly coincidental events, unrelated by cause and effect, but possessing deep significance for the observer. These events, connected by a "non-local intelligence," appear to be guided by this invisible web that interconnects everything in the universe.

The human mind, in its role as an active observer, can tune into this network of connections and, to some extent, access future events through intuition and sensitivity. The mind becomes a powerful tool of creation, influencing the possibilities that unfold in our reality.

Universal Synchronism, therefore, not only invites us to understand our innate connection with the cosmos but also urges us to explore the depths of our consciousness. By expanding our perception and embracing this intricate interconnection, we can live in greater harmony with the universe and with other human beings.

THE WISDOM OF UNIVERSAL SYNCHRONISM

The philosophy of Universal Synchronism teaches us that we are part of a cosmic web, where our actions and thoughts reverberate throughout the universe. By recognizing our intrinsic connection with all that exists, we are invited to act with compassion, empathy, and respect, acknowledging that each being and each event are intertwined in a harmonious dance of possibilities.

Ultimately, Universal Synchronism urges us to explore our inner potentials, recognizing that the human mind is an instrument of creation and manifestation of reality. By embracing this wisdom, we can tread a path of self-discovery and self-improvement, seeking synchronicity in our journey through the vast and mysterious universe.

TOXIC SYNCHRONICITY IN THE DIGITAL WORLD: THE CHALLENGE OF EVOLUTION

T

he digital world, an unprecedented human creation, has become a space for global interaction and information sharing. However, beneath the apparent connection and progress, a worrisome phenomenon has emerged: toxic synchronicity. In this context, negative and chaotic content seems to disproportionately attract our attention and engagement, while information about harmony, peace, and happiness is often overlooked.

This behavioral pattern raises important questions about how we use the digital world and its consequences on our society and collective well-being. The relentless pursuit of negative content can be attributed to psychological and social factors that influence our choices and online perceptions.

The human brain has a natural tendency to give greater importance to negative stimuli, as these stimuli can be perceived as threats to our safety and survival. Disasters, tragedies, and chaotic news activate alert mechanisms, provoking an immediate emotional response and a sense of urgency to share this information with others.

Furthermore, sharing negative news is faster and easier, contributing to its rapid spread on social networks. The immediate relevance of this content can also lead to the false impression that negative news is more important or more relevant than positive and constructive news.

Competitiveness and social comparison also play a significant role in this phenomenon. The digital world constantly exposes us to the successes and achievements of others, creating a mindset of scarcity and envy. The relentless pursuit of "likes" and interactions can lead to a vicious cycle, where success is measured in terms of popularity rather than intrinsic value or positive impact.

This relentless pursuit of negative content and constant comparison with others lead to "toxic synchronicity," where chaos and intolerance seem to prevail. The digital world becomes a space filled with discord, polarization, and sensationalism, where success metrics are often based on the number of interactions that negative content receives.

In the face of this scenario, it is essential to reflect on how we can adapt and use the potential of the digital world in a more constructive and evolutionary way. We must recognize that the pursuit of negative content and constant comparison does not lead us to significant evolution as intelligent beings.

We need to develop discernment and critical thinking skills regarding the content we consume. By becoming more aware of our choices and intentions when interacting in the digital world, we can avoid spreading false and harmful information.

Instead of being carried away by "toxic synchronicity," we can promote a healthier, empathetic, and harmonious online culture. Sharing positive news, promoting empathy, valuing genuine achievements, and recognizing the intrinsic value of each individual can be ways to reverse this trend and foster a more constructive and inspiring digital environment.

The digital world offers numerous possibilities for connectivity and learning. If we become more conscious and intentional in our choices, we can explore this virtual space to enhance our understanding of the world, promote collective evolution, and find meaning in the connections and interactions we build.

Thus, by moving away from "toxic synchronicity" and embracing a growth mindset, we can use the potential of the digital world to promote true evolution as intelligent beings and build a more promising and positive digital future for all. The path of evolution lies in our hands, and the choice is ours.

Transforming "Toxic Synchronicity" into Positive Evolution in the Digital Age

In the Digital Age, where interconnection among individuals is broader than ever, it is imperative to confront the challenge of "toxic synchronicity." This disturbing trend of giving more attention to negative, chaotic, and sensationalistic content in the digital world is negatively impacting our collective existence. However, by understanding our influence over Universal Synchronism, we can reprogram our minds and promote positive evolution in digital society.

The Foundation of Universal Synchronism

Universal Synchronism is the essence of interconnectedness of all things in the universe. It transcends time and space, linking us to every living being and phenomenon. Our thoughts, emotions, and actions are threads that weave this cosmic web, and understanding this interdependence is the starting point to shape a more constructive and harmonious digital environment.

EXPANSION OF CONSCIOUSNESS: A JOURNEY OF DISCOVERY

The key to reversing "toxic synchronicity" lies in the expansion of consciousness. Embracing the journey of discovering new perspectives, questioning limiting beliefs, and transcending the ego is essential to create a more positive digital presence. Empathy and compassion naturally arise when we connect to others' experiences and feelings, forming fertile ground for healthier coexistence.

REPROGRAMMING THE MIND FOR POSITIVITY

Reprogramming our minds is an ongoing process that requires self-discipline and self-compassion. We must acknowledge how our attention is captured by toxic content and make intentional choices to change this dynamic. By replacing the search for negative news with a desire to find constructive and inspiring information, we contribute to "positive synchronicity."

Becoming active creators of uplifting content inspires others to adopt a more constructive approach in the digital world. Sharing stories of hope, innovation, and social impact is a powerful means of contributing to a healthier and encouraging digital culture.

GRATITUDE AND SELF-CARE: PILLARS FOR DIGITAL WELL-BEING

Practicing gratitude helps us appreciate the achievements and success of others instead of feeling envy or threat. Cultivating a state of gratitude promotes positivity and enables us to resist the allure of toxic content, focusing on information that promotes well-being and personal growth.

Self-care is another essential pillar in this journey. Maintaining a balanced and healthy mind is crucial to facing the challenges of the digital world without being consumed by chaos. By taking care of ourselves, we become better prepared to promote positivity in our online interactions.

BUILDING A NEW DIGITAL REALITY

Each individual plays a fundamental role in building a new digital reality. By adopting a higher vision of connection and mutual understanding, we contribute to true collective evolution. By aligning our actions with this vision, we can promote a digital world more aligned with the higher potential of Universal Synchronism.

Change begins within each one of us. By being aware of our influence on Universal Synchronism and acting in accordance with that awareness, we create a more meaningful and positive digital environment for everyone. In this journey of transformation, our online interactions become an opportunity to promote healthier and more harmonious coexistence, reflecting true evolution in the Digital Age.

As we confront the challenge of "toxic synchronicity" in the Digital Age, we can rediscover the transformative potential of Universal Synchronism. By understanding our connection to the whole and reprogramming our minds through the expansion of consciousness, we hold the power to build a more uplifting and values-aligned digital world.

Together, we can shape a digital society that is more empathetic, harmonious, and positive, where each individual contributes to the creation of "positive synchronicity." This journey of collective evolution challenges us, but it also inspires us to harness the unlimited potential of the digital world to create a more meaningful and connected reality. Change begins within each of us, and it is at the intersection of Universal Synchronism and the Digital Age that we find the possibility of true and profound evolution.

EXPLORING PRACTICAL APPLICATIONS FOR THE THEORY OF UNIVERSAL SYNCHRONICITY IN EVERYDAY LIFE

The theory of Universal Synchronicity is not just a philosophical abstraction but also a practical approach to enhance our existence in the digital age and beyond. When discussing theoretical concepts, it is essential to provide readers with concrete examples of how they can incorporate these ideas into their daily lives to achieve a more positive and meaningful experience.

1. Interconnection Meditation: A meditation practice can be introduced, focused on the idea of interconnectedness among all beings and the universe. Readers are guided to reflect on their interdependence with the world around them, developing a deeper

sense of connection and empathy.

2. Digital Mindfulness: Offering guidance on practicing mindfulness while interacting with technology is crucial. Readers can be encouraged to be more aware of their online actions, take regular breaks, and evaluate the quality of their digital presence.

3. Empathy Exercises: Presenting practical exercises to develop empathy can help readers better understand others' perspectives and cultivate healthier relationships in the digital world. This may include practicing active listening and putting themselves in others' shoes.

4. Digital Gratitude: Encouraging the practice of gratitude in the digital environment is essential to counter the tendency to focus on negative things. Readers can be prompted to create specific gratitude lists for their digital experiences, acknowledging the meaningful

connections they encounter.

5. Awareness of Digital Impact: Encouraging reflection on the impact of our actions in the digital world is vital. Readers can be invited to consider how their posts, comments, and shares affect the online community and how they can be more mindful when expressing their opinions.

6. Digital Detox Practices: Discussing the importance of setting healthy boundaries for technology use and proposing digital detox activities can help readers balance their online presence with moments of self-care and connection with the offline world.

By providing concrete and practical examples of how to apply the theory of Universal Synchronicity in their everyday lives, the book empowers readers to effectively incorporate these principles into their actions and behaviors, fostering positive evolution in their relationship with the digital world and beyond. These practices can lead to greater harmony, empathy, and connection with the universe, resulting in a more meaningful existence aligned with the essence of Universal Synchronicity.

THE ERA OF CONSCIOUS EXPANSION OF UNIVERSAL SYNCHRONICITY

Through further study, experts in quantum physics, philosophy, psychology, and technology can significantly enrich the perspectives presented in the book "Universal Synchronicity in the Digital Age." By listening to the voices of experienced professionals in different fields, readers will be exposed to diverse and well-grounded views, deepening their understanding of the theory and its application in the context of the digital age.

There are several philosophers and thinkers who address the importance of surrounding oneself with positive people and connections in social settings. Some of them include:

Philosophers:

1. Aristotle: The Greek philosopher Aristotle believed in the importance of friendship and social relationships for a happy and virtuous life. He argued that friendship is essential for human well-being, and true friends are a source of emotional and intellectual support.

2. Epicurus: Epicurus, the Greek philosopher and founder of Epicureanism, emphasized the significance of friendship and harmonious interactions with others as fundamental components for attaining tranquility and happiness in life.

3. Confucius: Chinese thinker Confucius emphasized the importance of social relationships, ethics, and morality. He taught about the need to cultivate good interpersonal relationships based on compassion, respect, and responsibility.

4. Martin Buber: Jewish philosopher Martin Buber developed the philosophy of "I-Thou," which emphasizes the importance of authentic and meaningful connections with others. He advocated that genuine human connections are essential for a fulfilling and meaningful life.

5. Jean-Paul Sartre: French existentialist philosopher Sartre argued that intersubjectivity is an essential part of the human experience. He emphasized that human existence is inseparably linked to the existence of others, and our social relationships play a significant role in our identity and sense of self.

6. Simone de Beauvoir: French philosopher Simone de Beauvoir, also associated with existentialism, explored themes of freedom, responsibility, and interpersonal relationships. She emphasized the importance of taking responsibility

for our choices and relationships, seeking authenticity in connections with others.

These are just a few examples of philosophers who discussed the importance of surrounding oneself with positive people and connections in social settings. Each philosopher brings unique perspectives on the subject, but they all agree that our interpersonal relationships play a significant role in our life and well-being.

Quantum Physicists: Several quantum physicists have addressed the relationship between quantum physics and the human being, emphasizing interconnection and mutual influence in the universe. Some of these physicists include:

1. David Bohm: The theoretical physicist David Bohm developed an interpretation of quantum mechanics known as "Bohmian Mechanics" or the "Pilot-Wave

Theory." He argued that reality is fundamentally interconnected, and subatomic particles can be non-locally entangled, suggesting a deep interconnection in the fabric of the universe.

2. Fritjof Capra: Although not a quantum physicist himself, Fritjof Capra is a theoretical physicist who extensively wrote about the connections between quantum physics and spirituality. In his book "The Tao of Physics," he explores the similarities between quantum physics concepts and Eastern philosophies, emphasizing interconnectedness and the unity of all things.

3. Amit Goswami: Quantum physicist Amit Goswami is known for his contributions to the understanding of consciousness and spirituality from the perspective of quantum physics. He argues that consciousness is fundamental, and quantum physics can offer a new

understanding of the role of the mind in creating reality.

4. Nick Herbert: Theoretical physicist Nick Herbert has written about the connection between quantum physics and the human mind. In his book "Elemental Mind," he explores the possibility that the mind and consciousness may be linked to quantum phenomena in the brain.

5. Henry Stapp: Henry Stapp is a quantum physicist known for his work on the Copenhagen interpretation of quantum mechanics. He argues that the mind and consciousness play a fundamental role in quantum measurement, and reality is co-created by the observer and the observed.

These quantum physicists have varied perspectives on the relationship between quantum physics and the human being, but all explore the idea of interconnection and mutual influence in the universe. Their ideas challenge the traditional view of an objective reality and highlight the importance of consciousness and the mind in understanding the universe.

Psychologists: Some renowned psychologists specialized in consciousness and spirituality who offer perspectives on the relationship between the expansion of consciousness, spiritual practice, and the theory of Universal Synchronicity include:

1. Stanislav Grof: Stanislav Grof is a psychiatrist and psychotherapist known for his work with altered states of consciousness and transcendent experiences. He developed a therapeutic approach known as "Holotropic Breathwork," which uses breathing techniques and music to facilitate the

expansion of consciousness and access to deeper states of being.

2. Carl Jung: Although Carl Jung was not specifically a spiritual psychologist, he extensively explored the relationship between psychology and spirituality. Jung coined the term "synchronicity," which refers to meaningful and seemingly unrelated events that occur simultaneously, suggesting a deep connection between the mind and the universe.

3. Richard Alpert (Ram Dass): Richard Alpert, also known as Ram Dass, was a psychologist and spiritualist who studied the relationship between psychology and spirituality. After experiencing a shift in perspective during trips to India, he became an advocate for meditation, expansion of consciousness, and connection with universal spirituality.

4. Jack Kornfield: Jack Kornfield is a clinical psychologist and author

dedicated to the study of Buddhism and the practice of meditation. He explores the relationship between spirituality and mental well-being, arguing that meditation and spiritual practice can lead to a deeper connection with the universe and other human beings.

5. Rupert Sheldrake: Although primarily known as a biologist, Rupert Sheldrake also addresses issues related to consciousness and spirituality. He proposed the idea of "morphic resonance," which suggests an interconnectedness between all forms of life and mutual influence between individuals and the universe.

These psychologists have explored how the expansion of consciousness and spiritual practice can relate to the theory of Universal Synchronicity, highlighting how meditative practices and self-transformation can impact our connection with the universe and promote greater harmony and understanding of our existence.

Experts in Technology and Digital Behavior: Some renowned experts in Technology and Digital Behavior who have explored the challenges and opportunities of the digital age in relation to the theory of Universal Synchronicity include:

1. Sherry Turkle: Sherry Turkle is a professor and researcher at MIT who focuses on studying the interaction between humans and technology. She addresses issues such as device dependence, loneliness caused by excessive use of social media, and the effects of technology on interpersonal relationships. Turkle also explores the importance of genuine connection in a hyper-connected digital age and how we can use technology more consciously to

promote more meaningful relationships.

2. Tristan Harris: Tristan Harris is a former Google ethicist and the founder of the Center for Humane Technology. He advocates for conscious technology and ethics in the technology industry. Harris explores how social media and other digital platforms can manipulate our behavior and negatively influence our perception of reality. He promotes designing digital products and services that encourage positive and authentic connections, instead of exploiting addictive and harmful mechanisms.

3. Cal Newport: Cal Newport is a computer science professor and author who examines the effects of technology on productivity and mental well-being. In his books, he argues that the constant pursuit of notifications and excessive use of social media can compromise our ability to concentrate and be

creative. Newport proposes a more conscious approach to using technology, encouraging periods of disconnection and focus on meaningful activities.

4. Cathy O'Neil: Cathy O'Neil is a mathematician and author who explores the influence of algorithms and artificial intelligence in society. She addresses how digital technologies can reinforce biases and social inequalities, and how the pursuit of engagement on social media can lead to the spread of misinformation and polarization. O'Neil encourages the ethical and conscious use of technology to promote a fair and equitable society.

These renowned experts have contributed to the debate on the application of the theory of Universal Synchronicity in the digital age. They examine the challenges and opportunities presented by technology and how we can use these tools consciously to promote positive interconnection and avoid toxic synchronicity traps, seeking a more ethical and meaningful use of technology in our lives.

Reflections: Here are some deeper philosophical reflections on the nature of existence, the relationship between the mind and the universe, and how technology can affect our perception of reality:

1. Nature of Existence: Philosophy has always grappled with the fundamental question of the nature of existence. Universal Synchronicity suggests that everything in the universe is interconnected, transcending time and space. This interconnectedness leads us to question the separation between ourselves and the world around us. One can reflect on how our

perception of reality is shaped by our understanding of existence as a whole, and how the search for meaning and purpose may be influenced by this deep interconnectedness.

2. Relationship between Mind and Universe: Universal Synchronicity proposes that the human mind plays an active role in the manifestation of reality. Our perception and interpretation of events around us create our own reality framework. This leads us to question the nature of the mind and its relationship to the universe. One can explore how the mind, as a faculty of consciousness, can influence objective reality, and how our experiences and cognitions shape our understanding of the world.

3. Technology and Perception of Reality: The digital age has brought with it a wide range of technologies that shape our perception of reality.

Virtual reality, for example, can create immersive experiences that make us question what is real and what is simulated. Hyper-connectivity and the rapid dissemination of information through technology can also affect our understanding of truth and objective reality. In this context, it is essential to reflect on how technology can alter our perception of the world, both for better and for worse, and how we can use technology consciously to promote a more authentic and meaningful perception of reality.

4. Digital Awareness: Technology allows us to be constantly connected to the digital world, but this can also lead to information overload and constant distractions. One can reflect on how this constant digital connection affects our awareness and our ability to be present in the current moment. Digital awareness invites us to

question how to balance online and offline life and how to cultivate a more conscious and authentic awareness in a hyper-connected digital world.

These philosophical reflections on the nature of existence, the relationship between mind and universe, and the impact of technology on our perception of reality can enrich the understanding of Universal Synchronicity in the digital age. These questions challenge us to explore our own nature as conscious beings and how we can use technology ethically and consciously to promote a deeper and more meaningful understanding of the world around us.

SELF-ASSESSMENT TEST:

Conscious Interaction in the Digital Age

Instructions: Answer the following questions and mark the option that best describes your approach to interacting with the digital world and the challenges of the digital age.

Digital Presence: I am conscious and intentional when using technology to ensure that my digital presence reflects my identity and personal values.

a) I don't consider my digital presence consciously. b) Sometimes, I pay attention to my digital presence. c) I try to be mindful of how I present myself in the digital world. d) I am very conscious and intentional about my digital presence.

Digital Balance: I set healthy boundaries for the time spent in the digital world, ensuring a balance between online and offline life.

a) I have difficulty setting boundaries and spend a lot of time online. b) I try to find a balance, but sometimes, I find myself excessively involved in the digital world. c) I can establish reasonable limits and balance my online and offline presence. d) I am highly conscious and disciplined in maintaining a healthy balance.

Respect and Empathy Online: I practice respect and empathy when interacting with others in the digital environment, avoiding harmful behaviors.

a) Sometimes, I may engage in disrespectful or harmful online interactions. b) I try to be respectful and empathetic, but sometimes, I may make mistakes. c) I am conscious and intentional in my online interactions, always seeking to respect others. d) I always practice respect and empathy when interacting online and avoid harmful behaviors.

Digital Synchronicity: I use technology consciously to promote positive synchronicity and meaningful connections in the digital world.

a) I don't consider the importance of digital synchronicity in my online interactions. b) Sometimes, I try to create meaningful connections, but I am not always conscious of it. c) I am conscious and intentional in promoting digital synchronicity and creating meaningful connections. d) I am highly conscious and skillful in promoting digital synchronicity in all my interactions.

Digital Self-Care: I practice self-care in the digital world, protecting my mental and emotional well-being in relation to online content and interactions.

a) I don't pay much attention to my digital self-care and may be negatively affected by online content. b) I try to be more conscious, but sometimes, I find myself involved in stressful or harmful interactions. c) I am conscious and practice digital self-care, protecting my mental and emotional health. d) I am highly conscious and proactive in protecting my digital well-being, avoiding toxic content and negative interactions.

After answering these questions and assigning a score to each of them, add up the points and evaluate your conscious interaction in the digital age:

a: 0 points b: 1 point c: 2 points d: 3 points

Add up the points and evaluate your conscious interaction in the digital age:

0 to 5 points: There are significant opportunities to improve your conscious interaction in the digital world. Identify specific areas where you can work on developing a more conscious and healthy approach to technology.

6 to 10 points: You are on the right track, but there is still room for

improvement in your conscious interaction in the digital age. Continue to focus and practice a more mindful approach in your online activities.

11 to 15 points: Congratulations! You have demonstrated a highly conscious and balanced approach to the digital world. Continue to apply this awareness in all your online and offline interactions.

INTERCONNECTED AWARENESS

Instructions: Answer the following questions and mark the option that best describes your approach to interconnected awareness and your perception of the interconnection between all beings and events in the universe.

Understanding of Interconnection: I believe in the interconnection between all beings and events in the universe, recognizing that our actions and choices have an impact on a larger whole.

a) I don't consider the interconnection between beings and events in the universe. b) Sometimes, I reflect on the possibility of interconnection, but I don't fully understand it. c) I believe in interconnection and try to apply it in my life. d) I have a deep understanding of interconnection and apply this concept in all areas of my life.

Empathy and Compassion: I practice empathy and compassion in my interactions with others, recognizing that we are all part of an interconnected web of relationships.

a) I don't consider the importance of empathy and compassion in my interactions with others. b) I try to be empathetic and compassionate, but I don't always apply these principles consistently. c) I strive to be empathetic and compassionate in my interactions with others. d) I am highly empathetic and compassionate, always seeking to genuinely understand and support others.

Environmental Responsibility: I recognize my responsibility towards the environment and take steps to protect and preserve nature.

a) I don't consider my responsibility towards the environment. b) Sometimes, I try to take measures to protect the environment, but I don't consistently maintain them. c) I am conscious of my responsibility and take concrete measures to protect the environment. d) I am highly responsible and actively involved in environmental preservation.

Connection with the Community: I value connection with my community and seek to contribute positively to collective well-being.

a) I don't give much importance to connection with my community. b) Sometimes, I seek to connect with the community, but I am not always actively involved. c) I value connection with the community and seek to contribute to collective well-being. d) I am highly involved and committed to my community, always seeking to contribute meaningfully.

Awareness of Actions: I am aware of my actions and choices, seeking to align my decisions with the principles of interconnected awareness.

a) I don't pay much attention to my actions and choices. b) Sometimes, I reflect on my actions, but I don't always align them with interconnected awareness. c) I am aware of my actions and try to align them with the principles of interconnected awareness. d) I am highly conscious and committed to acting in accordance with the principles of interconnected awareness.

After answering these questions and assigning a score to each of them, add up the points and evaluate your interconnected awareness:

a: 0 points b: 1 point c: 2 points d: 3 points

Add up the points and evaluate your interconnected awareness:

0 to 5 points: There are significant opportunities to enhance your interconnected awareness. Identify specific areas where you can work to develop a more conscious and interconnected approach to life.

6 to 10 points: You are on the right track, but there is still room for improvement in your interconnected awareness. Continue to focus and practice a more conscious approach in your interactions with the world around you.

11 to 15 points: Congratulations! You have demonstrated a highly conscious and interconnected approach to life. Continue to apply this awareness in all your actions and choices, contributing to

a more harmonious and interconnected world.

DIGITAL AUTHENTICITY

Instructions: Answer the following questions and mark the option that best describes your authenticity and integrity when interacting and presenting yourself in the digital world.

Authentic Expression: I express myself authentically in the digital world, showing who I truly am without masks or false representations.

a) I don't feel comfortable expressing myself authentically, and I end up masking my true identity. b) I try to be authentic on some occasions, but I don't always feel at ease to be completely genuine. c) I make an effort to be authentic and honest in my interactions and presentations in the digital world. d) I am highly authentic and genuine in all my expressions and interactions in the digital environment.

Integrity in Publications: I maintain integrity in the information and content I share in the digital world, avoiding sharing false or misleading information.

a) I don't give much importance to the integrity of the information I share, and sometimes I may share dubious content. b) I try to be careful, but sometimes I may share information without fully verifying its accuracy. c) I am conscious and make an effort to share only accurate and reliable information. d) I am highly committed to the integrity and truthfulness of the information I share, ensuring that it is trustworthy.

Authentic Relationships: I seek to build authentic and meaningful relationships in the digital environment, cultivating genuine connections with other people.

a) I don't give much importance to relationships in the digital world, and I don't make an effort to build genuine connections. b) I try to be more authentic in my relationships, but I don't always manage to establish deep connections. c) I value authentic relationships and seek to cultivate them whenever possible. d) I am highly committed to building authentic and meaningful relationships with other people in the digital world.

Respect for Privacy: I respect the privacy of others in the digital world, avoiding intruding into their personal spaces or sharing private information without permission.

a) I don't pay much attention to the privacy of others and may inadvertently intrude into their personal spaces. b) I try to be more conscious of privacy, but I may make mistakes sometimes. c) I am respectful of people's privacy and take care not to intrude into their personal spaces. d) I am highly respectful and careful with the privacy of others, ensuring that their information is protected.

Honesty in Interactions: I am honest in my interactions in the digital world, avoiding creating false personas or distorting information about myself.

a) I don't feel comfortable being honest in my interactions and end up creating false personas. b) I try to be more honest, but I may sometimes exaggerate or distort information about myself. c) I am honest most of the time in my interactions and avoid creating false personas. d) I am highly honest and genuine in all my interactions, always seeking to present myself as I truly am.

After answering these questions and assigning a score to each of them, add up the points and evaluate your digital authenticity:

a: 0 points b: 1 point c: 2 points d: 3 points

Add up the points and evaluate your digital authenticity:

0 to 5 points: There are significant opportunities to enhance your digital authenticity. Identify specific areas where you can work to be more genuine and authentic in your online interactions and presentations.

6 to 10 points: You are on the right track, but there is still room for improvement in your digital authenticity. Continue to focus and practice the genuine expression of yourself in the digital world.

11 to 15 points: Congratulations! You have demonstrated a highly authentic and integral approach in the digital world. Continue to apply this authenticity in all your interactions and online content, creating meaningful connections with others.

DIGITAL RESILIENCE

Instructions: Answer the following questions and mark the option that best describes your digital resilience in the face of challenges and adversities encountered in the digital environment.

Adaptation to New Technologies: I easily adapt to new technologies and digital platforms that emerge in the online scene.

a) I have difficulty adapting to new technologies and prefer to stick with what I'm already familiar with. b) I can adapt, but it usually takes time for me to feel comfortable with new technologies. c) I am reasonably agile in adapting to new technologies and digital platforms. d) I am highly adaptable and quickly familiarize myself with new technologies.

Online Change Management: I effectively deal with changes in online environments, such as policy updates, algorithms, or website layouts.

a) I have difficulty dealing with online changes and may become stressed or confused. b) I can adapt to changes, but it usually takes time for me to adjust. c) I am able to handle online changes reasonably well, but I may sometimes feel resistant. d) I am highly resilient in relation to online changes and see them as opportunities for growth.

Overcoming Digital Obstacles: I effectively deal with obstacles and digital challenges that I encounter, such as technical issues or online conflicts.

a) I have difficulty overcoming digital obstacles and may get frustrated or give up easily. b) I can overcome some digital obstacles, but not always with ease. c) I am resilient most of the time and find solutions to most digital challenges. d) I am highly resilient and capable of dealing with any digital obstacle that arises.

Recovery from Digital Errors: I easily recover from mistakes I make in the digital environment, learning from them and moving forward.

a) I have difficulty recovering from digital errors and may feel embarrassed or guilty. b) I can recover from some errors, but sometimes I dwell on the situation. c) I am able to recover from digital errors, learning from them and moving forward. d) I am highly resilient in relation to digital errors and don't let them affect me.

Frustration and Tolerance: I maintain calmness and tolerance in the face of frustrating situations that may arise in the digital environment.

a) I have difficulty controlling my frustration and may react negatively. b) I can remain calm most of the time, but sometimes I feel bothered. c) I am reasonably tolerant and can handle most frustrating situations. d) I am highly tolerant and patient, even in digitally challenging situations.

After answering these questions and assigning a score to each of them, add up the points and evaluate your digital resilience:

a: 0 points b: 1 point c: 2 points d: 3 points

Add up the points and evaluate your digital resilience:

0 to 5 points: There are significant opportunities to improve your digital resilience. Identify specific areas where you can work to become more adaptable and resilient in the face of online challenges.

6 to 10 points: You are on the right track, but there is still room for improvement in your digital resilience. Continue to focus and practice overcoming obstacles and online changes.

11 to 15 points: Congratulations! You have demonstrated high digital

resilience. Continue applying this skill to deal with the challenges and adversities encountered in the digital environment.

Conscious Use of Social Media

Instructions: Answer the following questions and mark the option that best describes your use of social media and how you approach this form of digital interaction.

Awareness of Online Time: I am conscious of the time I spend on social media and avoid staying connected for long periods without a clear purpose.

a) I don't pay much attention to the time spent on social media and can spend hours without realizing it. b) Sometimes, I find myself losing track of time on social media, but I try to limit my use. c) I am aware of my online time and try to use social media with a defined purpose. d) I am highly conscious of the time I spend on social media and maintain a balanced use.

Positive and Meaningful Content: I seek to consume and share content that is positive, informative, and meaningful to me and others.

a) I don't pay much attention to the type of content I consume or share. b) I try to consume and share positive content, but I don't always do it consistently. c) I consciously seek to consume and share positive and meaningful content. d) I am highly selective with the content I consume and share, prioritizing what is positive and relevant.

Conscious Interaction: I am conscious and intentional when interacting with others on social media, promoting respect and empathy.

a) I don't pay much attention to how I interact on social media and can be impulsive in my responses. b) I try to be more mindful in my interactions, but sometimes I may react emotionally. c) I am conscious and intentional in promoting respect and empathy in my online interactions. d) I am highly aware and empathetic in my interactions on social media, avoiding unnecessary conflicts.

Privacy Preservation: I take measures to protect my privacy and the privacy of others when sharing information on social media.

a) I don't worry much about my privacy and share personal information without much caution. b) I try to be more careful with my privacy, but sometimes I end up sharing sensitive information. c) I am conscious and proactive in protecting my privacy and avoid sharing delicate information. d) I am highly conscious and diligent in protecting my privacy and the privacy of others.

Conscious Disconnection: I take conscious breaks from social media when necessary to avoid overload or excessive dependence.

a) I don't usually take breaks from social media and find it difficult to disconnect. b) I try to take breaks, but I can't always stay away from social media for long. c) I am capable of disconnecting from social media when necessary to preserve my digital well-being. d) I am highly aware of the importance of taking regular breaks and enjoying the present moment.

After answering these questions and assigning a score to each of them, add up the points and evaluate your conscious use of social media:

a: 0 points b: 1 point c: 2 points d: 3 points

Add up the points and evaluate your conscious use of social media:

0 to 5 points: There are significant opportunities to improve your conscious use of social media. Identify specific areas where you can work to develop a more balanced and positive approach to social media.

6 to 10 points: You are on the right track, but there is still room for improvement in your conscious use of social media. Continue to focus and practice a more mindful approach to your online activities.

11 to 15 points: Congratulations! You have demonstrated a high level of awareness in the use of social media. Continue applying this conscious approach in your interactions and sharing online.

DIGITAL EMPATHY

Instructions: Answer the following questions and mark the option that best describes your ability to demonstrate empathy in your digital interactions.

Understanding Others' Emotions: I am capable of perceiving and understanding the emotions of others with whom I interact online.

a) I have difficulty perceiving others' emotions and often misinterpret their messages. b) I try to be more attentive, but sometimes I may not fully grasp others' emotions. c) I am able to perceive and understand the emotions of most people with whom I interact online. d) I am highly empathetic and can easily understand others' emotions.

Respect for Differences and Opinions: I respect different opinions and perspectives from mine when interacting with others in the digital environment.

a) I have difficulty accepting different opinions and can be intolerant towards those who think differently from me. b) I try to be more open, but sometimes I may feel uncomfortable with opposing viewpoints. c) I am respectful most of the time, but I may have difficulties with very divergent opinions. d) I am highly respectful and embrace differences of opinions, valuing the diversity of thoughts.

Empathy in Digital Conflicts: I demonstrate empathy even in situations of conflict or disagreement online.

a) I have difficulty maintaining empathy during conflicts and may respond aggressively. b) I try to be more empathetic, but sometimes I get involved in emotional discussions. c) I am empathetic most of the time, but I may encounter difficulties during tense moments. d) I am highly empathetic and can remain calm and understanding even in conflictual situations.

Support and Comfort Online: I offer support and comfort to people going through difficult times on social media and the internet.

a) I rarely offer support or comfort, and I may not know how to help others online. b) I try to be more supportive, but sometimes I don't know how to express my support adequately. c) I offer support and comfort to people in need most of the time, but sometimes I may struggle to find the right words. d) I am highly supportive and effective in offering support and comfort to people facing difficulties online.

Practicing Active Listening: I practice active listening, genuinely paying attention to the people with whom I interact online.

a) I have difficulty practicing active listening and often get easily distracted. b) I try to be more attentive, but sometimes I may not give the proper attention during digital conversations. c) I practice active listening most of the time, but I may improve my concentration skills. d) I am highly attentive and practice active listening efficiently during my digital interactions.

After answering these questions and assigning a score to each of them, add up the points and evaluate your digital empathy:

a: 0 points b: 1 point c: 2 points d: 3 points

Add up the points and evaluate your digital empathy:

0 to 5 points: There are significant opportunities to improve your digital empathy and ability to emotionally connect with others online. Identify specific areas where you can work to develop a more empathetic and understanding approach in your digital interactions.

6 to 10 points: You are on the right track, but there is still room for improvement in your digital empathy. Continue to focus and practice a more empathetic approach in your online activities.

11 to 15 points: Congratulations! You have demonstrated a high level of digital empathy and genuinely connect emotionally with others. Continue applying this empathy in all your online

interactions to create meaningful connections.

DIGITAL MINDFULNESS

Instructions: Answer the following questions and mark the option that best describes your practice of mindfulness in the use of digital technologies.

Awareness of Excessive Use: I am aware when I am spending too much time using digital devices and browsing the internet.

a) I don't pay much attention to the time I spend on digital devices. b) Sometimes, I realize that I am spending too much time online, but I don't always take measures to reduce it. c) I am aware and make efforts to limit my excessive use of digital devices. d) I am highly aware and disciplined in balancing my time between the digital and offline world.

Mindful Attention in Online Interactions: I practice mindful attention during my interactions with other people in the digital environment.

a) I rarely practice mindful attention during online interactions and can easily get distracted. b) I try to be more attentive, but sometimes I engage in other activities at the same time. c) I am attentive most of the time, but I can improve my focus in some situations. d) I am highly attentive and practice mindful attention during my digital interactions.

Breaks for Recharging: I take conscious breaks throughout the day to rest from digital devices and relax my mind.

a) I rarely take conscious breaks and may feel mentally exhausted. b) I try to take breaks, but sometimes I find myself stuck in online activities for long periods. c) I take conscious breaks most of the time, but I may occasionally forget. d) I am highly aware and take regular breaks to recharge my mind and body.

Digital Impulse Control: I have control over the impulse to constantly check notifications and social media.

a) I have difficulty controlling the impulse and often feel compelled to check notifications. b) I try to be more conscious, but sometimes I am tempted to check social media unnecessarily. c) I can control most of the time, but sometimes I give in to the impulse to check. d) I am highly aware and disciplined in controlling the impulse to constantly check.

Mindful of Online Content: I am selective and conscious about the type of content I consume online, prioritizing useful and healthy information.

a) I am not very selective and consume a wide variety of content without much thought about its quality. b) I try to be more mindful, but sometimes end up consuming content that is not relevant or healthy. c) I am selective most of the time, but I can improve in choosing more useful and healthy content. d) I am highly aware and proactive in consuming online content that is relevant and beneficial.

After answering these questions and assigning a score to each of them, add up the points and evaluate your practice of digital mindfulness:

a: 0 points b: 1 point c: 2 points d: 3 points

Add up the points and evaluate your practice of digital mindfulness:

0 to 5 points: There are significant opportunities to improve your practice of digital mindfulness and develop a greater awareness of the use of technologies. Identify specific areas where you can work to cultivate more mindfulness in your online activities.

6 to 10 points: You are on the right track, but there is still room for improvement in your practice of digital mindfulness. Continue to focus and

practice mindful attention in your online activities.

11 to 15 points: Congratulations! You have demonstrated a solid practice of digital mindfulness and are aware of how you use technologies. Continue applying this mindfulness to have a healthier and more balanced relationship with the digital world.

DIGITAL BALANCE AND OFFLINE LIFE

Instructions: Answer the following questions and mark the option that best describes the balance between digital use and your offline life.

Disconnection Time: I regularly set aside time to disconnect from digital devices and engage in offline activities.

a) I rarely set aside time to disconnect and constantly feel attached to digital devices. b) I try to disconnect occasionally, but I don't always do it consistently. c) I reserve time to disconnect most of the time, but I may occasionally forget. d) I am disciplined in setting aside time to disconnect and value my offline life as much as my digital life.

Meaningful Offline Activities: I regularly engage in offline activities that I consider meaningful and enriching.

a) I rarely engage in meaningful offline activities and often feel bored. b) I try to engage in offline activities, but I don't always find meaningful things to do. c) I engage in meaningful offline activities most of the time, but I can improve the variety of options. d) I am highly aware and creative in engaging in activities offline that I consider meaningful.

Relationships and Personal Connections: I prioritize personal relationships and face-to-face interactions instead of relying solely on digital interactions.

a) Many of my social interactions are only online, and I rarely prioritize in-person meetings. b) I try to balance online and offline interactions, but sometimes I rely too much on digital platforms. c) I value personal relationships, but I also recognize the importance of digital interactions. d) I prioritize personal interactions and value face-to-face connections above exclusively digital interactions.

Awareness of Offline Well-being: I am aware of my emotional and mental well-being in the offline environment and seek to take care of myself in this area.

a) I rarely pay attention to my offline well-being and may neglect my feelings and emotional needs. b) I try to be more aware of my well-being, but I don't always prioritize taking care of myself. c) I am aware of my offline well-being most of the time, but I can improve on self-reflection. d) I am highly aware and proactive in taking care of my emotional and mental well-being offline.

Integration of Digital and Offline: I integrate digital technologies into my offline life in a balanced way, using them to complement my activities and interests.

a) I rarely integrate the digital world into my offline life and see these two areas as separate. b) I try to find integration, but I don't always manage to balance the two areas properly. c) Integrating the digital and offline is something I do most of the time, but I can improve this skill. d) I am highly aware and skilled at integrating the digital and offline in a balanced and harmonious way.

After answering these questions and assigning a score to each of them, add up the points and evaluate your digital balance and offline life:

a: 0 points b: 1 point c: 2 points d: 3 points

Add up the points and evaluate your digital balance and offline life:

0 to 5 points: There are significant opportunities to improve the balance between the digital and offline life. Identify specific areas where you can work to develop a more balanced relationship between these two areas.

6 to 10 points: You are on the right track, but there is still room for improvement in your digital balance and offline life. Continue to focus and practice a more balanced approach to the use of technologies.

11 to 15 points: Congratulations! You have demonstrated a high level of digital balance and offline life. Continue applying this balance to have a healthy and meaningful relationship with the digital and offline world.□

POSITIVE IMPACT IN THE DIGITAL AGE

Instructions: Answer the following questions and mark the option that best describes the positive impact you seek to create in the digital age.

Digital Purpose and Contribution: I seek to use my digital presence to positively contribute to others, offering meaningful value and knowledge.

a) I rarely consider my digital purpose and don't worry about contributing positively. b) I try to offer value, but I'm not always aware of how I can contribute meaningfully. c) I am conscious and intentional in offering valuable contributions to others in the digital age. d) I actively seek to create a positive and significant impact, sharing enriching knowledge and experiences.

Digital Empowerment: I seek to empower others to use technology in a positive and responsible manner to improve their lives.

a) I rarely consider the digital empowerment of others and don't get involved in this area. b) I try to encourage others, but I don't always know how to help them empower themselves digitally. c) I am conscious and intentional in empowering others to use technology positively. d) I actively seek to empower others, guiding them on responsible and beneficial technology use.

Digital Inclusion and Diversity: I strive to create an inclusive digital environment where everyone feels respected and represented.

a) I rarely consider the importance of digital inclusion and diversity in my online interactions. b) I try to be more aware, but I'm not always attentive to inclusion and diversity issues. c) I am conscious and intentional in creating an inclusive and respectful digital environment. d) I actively promote digital inclusion and diversity, advocating for equitable representation of all voices.

Social Impact Initiatives: I participate in or support social impact initiatives in the digital age, seeking to make a difference in people's lives and communities.

a) I rarely get involved in social impact initiatives and don't see the connection between technology and social change. b) I try to support causes, but I don't always find social impact initiatives aligned with my interests. c) I am conscious and intentional in supporting impactful initiatives that make a difference. d) I actively participate in and promote social impact initiatives, using technology as a tool for positive change.

Digital Responsibility: I take responsibility for my actions and words in the digital environment, avoiding disseminating harmful or false information.

a) I rarely worry about digital responsibility and may share information without verifying its accuracy. b) I try to be more conscious, but I'm not always aware of the impact of my online actions. c) I am conscious and intentional in being responsible in my interactions and information sharing. d) I actively seek to be a reliable and responsible source in the digital environment, promoting the dissemination of accurate and useful information.

After answering these questions and assigning a score to each of them, add up the points and evaluate your positive impact in the digital age:

a: 0 points b: 1 point c: 2 points d: 3 points

Add up the points and evaluate your positive impact in the digital age:

0 to 5 points: There are significant opportunities to improve your positive

impact in the digital age. Identify specific areas where you can work to create a more significant and beneficial impact.

6 to 10 points: You are on the right track, but there is still room for improvement in your positive impact in the digital age. Continue to focus and practice actions that contribute to a more positive and inclusive digital environment.

11 to 15 points: Congratulations! You have demonstrated a high level of positive impact in the digital age. Continue applying your influence to make a difference and create a better digital environment for everyone.

CULTIVATING HEALTHY DIGITAL RELATIONSHIPS

Instructions: Answer the following questions and mark the option that best describes how you cultivate healthy relationships in the digital environment.

Authenticity and Transparency: I am authentic and transparent in my online interactions, expressing my true personality and opinions.

a) I rarely show authenticity or transparency, preferring to maintain an idealized image. b) I try to be more authentic, but sometimes hesitate to express my true opinion. c) I am conscious and intentional about being authentic most of the time. d) I am completely authentic and transparent, acting with sincerity in all my online interactions.

Respect for Differences: I respect the opinions and perspectives different from my own, avoiding unnecessary conflicts and promoting constructive dialogue.

a) I rarely consider the importance of respecting differences and may be intolerant in some situations. b) I try to be more aware, but I may engage in heated debates at times. c) I am conscious and intentional about respecting differences and seeking mutual understanding. d) I actively seek to promote empathy and respect, valuing the diversity of opinions.

Boundaries and Privacy: I establish clear boundaries regarding my privacy and respect the boundaries of others in the digital environment.

a) I rarely consider the importance of boundaries and privacy, sharing personal information without much thought. b) I try to be more conscious, but sometimes find myself in situations that compromise my privacy or that of others. c) I am conscious and intentional about establishing healthy boundaries and respecting everyone's privacy. d) I am highly conscious and protective of my privacy and the privacy of others in the digital environment.

Empathetic Communication: I practice empathy and care when communicating with others, showing understanding and support when needed.

a) I rarely worry about being empathetic in my communications and may come across as insensitive. b) I try to be more empathetic, but I'm not always able to demonstrate genuine understanding. c) I am conscious and intentional about practicing empathy in most of my online interactions. d) I actively strive to be a source of support and understanding, offering empathy and care in my communications.

Conflict and Resolution: I deal with conflicts in the digital environment constructively, seeking to resolve misunderstandings in a respectful manner.

a) I rarely engage in conflicts or avoid resolving misunderstandings. b) I try to deal with conflicts, but I may not always approach them constructively. c) I am conscious and intentional about handling conflicts in a respectful manner and seeking peaceful solutions. d) I am highly skilled in resolving conflicts and promoting mutual understanding in the digital environment.

After answering these questions and assigning a score to each of them, add up the points and evaluate your cultivation of healthy digital relationships:

a: 0 points b: 1 point c: 2 points d: 3 points

Add up the points and evaluate your cultivation of healthy digital relationships:

0 to 5 points: There are significant opportunities to improve cultivating healthy relationships in the digital environment. Identify specific areas where you can work to develop more authentic and empathetic interactions.

6 to 10 points: You are on the right track, but there is still room for improvement in cultivating healthy digital relationships. Continue to focus and

practice behaviors that strengthen your bonds in the online world.

11 to 15 points: Congratulations! You have demonstrated a high level of skill in cultivating healthy digital relationships. Continue applying this empathetic and authentic approach in all your online interactions.

Conclusion

In this exciting journey, we have explored the mysteries of the Quantum Revolution and how it impacts our perception of reality. We have understood that the pursuit of metrics and understanding of this new reality is essential for conscious and positive evolution.

As we ventured into the universe of Universal Synchronicity, we discovered the profound interconnection between the mind and the cosmos. We explored the quantum foundations of this theory, such as decoherence and synchronicity, which teach us to co-create our own reality.

Never has it been so crucial to comprehend and apply the principles of Universal Synchronicity in the digital age. We face an avalanche of information and daily technological challenges, and it is in this scenario that

Universal Synchronicity stands out as a compass to navigate complex waters.

By internalizing the concepts of this book, we gain valuable tools to deal with the challenges of the digital age. The expansion of consciousness allows us to transcend boundaries, while cultivating authenticity, resilience, and digital empathy makes us positive agents of change.

I invite every reader to pause in this frenetic moment of digital life and reflect on their attitudes and choices. Let us look at our interactions on social media, the impact we cause and receive. How are we managing our digital balance and mental health?

May this invitation to reflection be a seed for change. I encourage each one to apply the teachings of this book and embark on a journey of growth and self-discovery in the digital age.

At the core of Universal Synchronicity, we find hope and inspiration. We are co-creators of reality, connected by invisible threads that transcend the digital world. We can positively impact our own lives and that of others, propagating a wave of meaningful change.

Trust in the transformative power of Universal Synchronicity. There are no limits to the expansion of consciousness, and together, we can shape a more harmonious and connected future.

Acknowledgments:

To our families, friends, and mentors, we express our deep gratitude for supporting and inspiring this project. Without your encouragement, dedication, and love, this book would not be possible.

And finally, to the readers who dedicated their time to reading this work, our sincerest gratitude. We hope you have been touched by the ideas presented and carry with you the

principles of Universal Synchronicity on
your   journeys.

Author's Biography:

Katia Doria Fonseca Vasconcelos is a multifaceted professional, passionate about the balance between technology, personal development, and quality of life. With a background in Systems Analysis and solid experience in the Information Technology (IT) field, Katia stands out as a visionary in the digital universe and the application of Universal Synchronicity in the digital age.

Since the beginning of her career, Katia has understood the importance of enhancing human behavior and quality of life, in addition to technical knowledge. Her professional journey and relentless pursuit of new possibilities have led her to explore the profound interconnection between the mind and the universe, and how it applies to the digital world.

As the author of the book "Universal Synchronicity in the Digital Age," Katia takes readers on a journey of discovery about how the principles of Universal Synchronicity can be applied in the context of the digital age. Her book addresses relevant topics such as interconnected consciousness, digital authenticity, resilience in the virtual environment, and the cultivation of healthy digital relationships.

With engaging storytelling, Katia highlights the importance of understanding and applying these principles in the digital age to enhance our experience and well-being in this increasingly interconnected environment. The book is an invitation to reflection, encouraging readers to contemplate their own attitudes and behaviors towards technology, and to implement conscious practices for a more positive and meaningful digital experience.

As an inspiring voice, Katia shares her wisdom and transformative vision, offering a message of hope to face the challenges of the digital age with balance, empathy, and respect. Her work reflects a commitment to promoting digital awareness and cultivating a more fulfilling and connected life at the intersection of technology and personal well-being.

With "Universal Synchronicity in the Digital Age," Katia Doria Fonseca Vasconcelos solidifies herself as an author who seeks to explore new horizons, positively impacting the lives of her readers by exploring synchronicity and harmony between the digital world and the human essence.

www.ingramcontent.com/pod-product-compliance
Lightning Source LLC
Chambersburg PA
CBHW062329290526
45794CB00005B/1965